HUMILITY

Master Key to Unlocking
Your God-given Destiny

by

SHELIA A. SMITH

DEDICATION

First and foremost, I dedicate this book to the Holy Spirit, because He is my Senior Partner and the One who planted the seed in me to write my very first book back in August 1998. The seed seemed to lay dormant for a while, but at the appointed time, the germination process began, and *Simply Faith*, the first book, was birthed October 2017. And now, the time has come forth for the birthing of *Humility: Master Key to Unlocking Your God-Given Destiny*, which is the first of seven books in the series. Why now? Because it is the appointed season for the glory of God to be revealed in me and through me for his name's sake.

Secondly, I dedicate this book to the late Miss Lottie, my mama, the wind who is still beneath my wings. I am sure she is peering over the banisters of heaven with the great cloud of witnesses cheering me on. She taught me first to love God, and then to put my trust in Him and Him alone.

And last but not least, I dedicate this book to my two sons, Roderick and Oliver Jr., the reason that I continue to press toward the mark for the prize of the high calling of God in Christ Jesus to be an example and a living legacy of the Father's love and His faithfulness.

SPECIAL RECOGNITION TO:

My dearest and close friends and mentors; you know who you are!

And, I would be remiss to not personally make mention of apostle Dr. Oscar G., who encouraged me to keep writing through a prophetic word that I received from him on 6/28/2019, the last day of our online class. "Shelia, the Lord said, 'Write again…' I don't know what you do, but the Lord said to tell you, 'Write again, Shelia, write again.'"

CONTENTS

Foreword

From what I've been told, a Foreword is typically written by someone who is influential and can lend credibility to the book. My thoughts haven't changed since I wrote and published my first book, *Simply Faith: The Birthing of a Warrior* in 2017. The Most Important Person on Earth: The Holy Spirit, the heavenly Governor, is my Senior Partner, and once again approves the writing of my second book: *Humility: Master Key to Unlocking Your God-given Destiny*. Why this book? This book is the first of seven books in a series addressing Christian character and virtues we should exhibit as children of God if we are to walk and live out our God-given destiny. Therefore, my desire is to help Christian and "Pre-Christian" women (those who are yet to answer His call) who love the Lord and have a desire to fulfill their destiny and calling in life but they don't know their purpose; don't know how to discover their gifts and passions.

They are either stuck, have a fear of failure, fear of taking risks, and/or fear of rejection because they are people pleasers instead of God pleasers.

We as Christians are to do the work of the ministry; we are to bear good fruit because Jesus said those that believe in Him will be able to do greater works than He did because He is going to His Father (John 14:12).

Why now? "The harvest is plentiful, but the laborers are few." (Matt. 9:37) ESV. The captives are crying out to be set free, but if the laborers are unaware of who they are, or are untrained or unskilled, they will, therefore, be unavailable. The Bible says, "It is expedient that I do the works of him that sent me while it is day; the night comes when no one can work" John 9:4 (Jubilee 2000). I must take my rightful place now, while it is yet daylight! I must work to help equip God's women so we can work together in advancing the kingdom of God for His glory to be revealed in us and through us for His name's sake. The time is **NOW!** The Lord has said, "Shelia, write again!" This book is not a minute too soon nor a minute too late—God's timing!

Introduction

Break open your word within me until revelation-light shines out! Those with open hearts are given insight into your plans. I open my mouth and inhale the word of God because I crave the revelation of your commands.

— Psalms 119:130–131 The Passion Translation

As I sit here praying and asking the Holy Spirit (the most important Person on Earth) for guidance, I can't think of a better way to discern or comprehend the plans, purpose, and destiny God has for our lives without having a personal relationship with Him, through His written Word and then personal encounters. I am forever grateful to my Mama Lottie, adoptive grandparents (Bishop Elijah Sr. and Mother Aileen Banks), who are all gone home to be with the Lord Jesus and my spiritual mother, Imelda, who faithfully, year after year, encouraged and sometimes insisted that I get to know Jesus for myself through his written Word.

God has a plan, and there is a God-given destiny that he preordained for each of us before the foundations of the world. (Jer. 29:11). I believe that one will never be able to fulfill his or her God-given destiny outside of a personal relationship with God. "For since the creation of the world God's invisible qualities—his eternal power and divine nature—have been clearly seen, being understood from what has been made, so that men are without excuse" (Rom. 1:20; Ps. 19:1–4; Acts 14:17). God also reveals Himself through what is called special revelation through physical appearances of Himself, dreams, visions, the written *Word* of God, and through His Son, Jesus Christ (Gen. 3:8, 18:1, Exod. 3:1–4, Ezek. 1–2, 2 Cor. 12:1–7). And most importantly is His written Word (Heb. 4:12, and 2 Tim. 3:16–17), which teaches us what is right, what is wrong, how to get it right, and how to keep it right.

I am reminded of a reflection paper that I wrote after reading the book *Visioneering* by Dr. Andy

Stanley as part of the requirements for my Christian Professional Life Coaching Certification. The author stated, "Life is a journey, and every journey has a destination." And more importantly, every person God created will end up somewhere in life. However, as the author stated, "A few people end up somewhere on purpose." The word *purpose* captured my attention because that had been the cry of my heart to the Lord; it seems for years. I genuinely wanted to know what my purpose is. Why am I here? What was I created to do? In other words, God, what is your plan for my life? What is my God-given destiny?

I imagine you picked up a copy of this book because you most likely have some of the same questions I did. Listen to what the author said, "The average person has the right to dream his own dreams and develop his picture of what his future could and should be." However, this is not the case for those of us who confess Jesus Christ as our Lord and Savior. The Bible is clear that "We are his workmanship created in Christ Jesus for good works, which God prepared **beforehand so that we would walk in them**"

Emphasis mine (Eph. 2:10 New King James Version). In other words, if we want to know what our God-given destiny is, then we must go to the Source.

In my first book, *Simply Faith: The Birthing of a Warrior*, I share a few testimonies of personal encounters with God as I learned to trust Him through his Word, even amid my darkest seasons. I learned—and I am still learning—that God's Word is truth and cannot return unto Him void. It will accomplish everything that He pleases and will prosper in the thing for which He sent it (Isa. 55:11 NKJV). I also shared that I believe there are seven keys to living a life filled with purpose, and it begins with faith in God and His Word.

In this short read, my goal is to elaborate on humility from a biblical view of what I believe is the first key to unlocking your God-given destiny. I am not claiming to have arrived. However, I will share valuable, life-changing principles that I learned as the Holy Spirit walked me through the dark nights of my soul. My twenty-five-year marriage ending in divorce; then, less than 10 months later, I lost my job of 18½ years; and if that wasn't enough, my health became an issue as I went from bodybuilding and running marathons to struggling with vertigo (dizzy spells) that lasted for almost three years without any answer as to why.

I have been up, and I have been down, but I have never been without. God has positioned me right in the middle of His will and plan for my life. I have grown (and I'm still growing) spiritually, personally, socially, professionally, and financially, and would love to show you how God will do the same thing for you too.

The one thing I have learned without any doubt is that I can do nothing good outside of Christ. If I have done anything noble, it is because of Him. "For it is God who works in me both to will and to do for his good pleasure" (Phil. 2:13). I am a witness that "…all things work together for good to those who love God, to those who are called according to his purpose" (Rom. 8:32).

My prayer is that this book goes beyond the Church, meaning that it is not written ONLY for those who profess Jesus Christ as Lord and Savior. The Scripture declares that if we receive God's Son and believe in his name, then we are his children. "But as many as received Him, to them He gave the right to become children of God, to those who believe in His name who were born, not of blood, nor of the will of the flesh, nor of the will of man, but of God" (Jn. 1:12–13). However, Jesus also stated, "There are other sheep I have which are not of this fold, them also, I must bring, and they will hear My voice, and there will be one flock and one shepherd" (Jn. 10:16).

So, as a disciple of Jesus Christ, it is my heart's desire that everyone who is not of the fold at this time after or during the reading of this book will respond to His voice as the Scripture exhorts: "Today, if you would hear His voice, Do not harden your hearts, as in the rebellion, as in the day of trial in the wilderness…" (Ps. 95:8). This passage is referring to the Israelites (God's special people) who heard his voice, but were in unbelief; therefore, they did not enter into his rest (Ps. 95:11).

God is merciful, but sadly, there are still some people today who are prideful (the very opposite of humility), who refuse to humble themselves and acknowledge him for who he is. God's loving-kindness is from everlasting to everlasting to those who reverence him, and his salvation is to the children's children to those who are faithful to his covenant and remember to obey him (Ps. 103:17–18 The Living Bible).

He has provided the opportunity to become his child by accepting the gift of salvation that comes only through His Son, Jesus Christ. He has not left us (his most prized creation) defenseless and wondering how to live a life surrendered unto Him. The Bible declares we can boldly ask God for wisdom, and He won't scold us or hold our lack of wisdom against us. Instead, He will "overwhelm our failures with his generous grace" (Jas. 1:5 TPT). Go ahead and try Him for yourself. If you lack wisdom, just ask Him! The book of Proverbs recounts numerous passages that contrast the wise man and the foolish man. Proverbs 14:8 states, "For the wisdom of the wise will keep life on the right track, while the fool only deceives himself and refuses to face reality." Perhaps this may be your first time dedicating your life to Christ, or you may be "re-dedicating" your life to the Savior; either way, please take this moment to pause right where you are and act while you have the opportunity.

❖ *Reflections*

Reflect on these questions and journal your thoughts/experiences.

Do you have a personal relationship with Jesus Christ, the Son of God, the Savior of the world? Do you consider yourself to be the "wise man" or the "foolish man?" There is a difference between worldly wisdom and godly wisdom. Do you lack Godly wisdom? (Jas. 3:15–17). From this passage, what is the difference? Do you desire Godly wisdom? If so, read James 1:5 and pray this simple prayer with a sincere heart: "Father God, I thank you that I have prayed the Prayer of Salvation (at the end of this book) and have received Jesus in my heart as Lord and Savior. I am your child, and thank you that I can come boldly to the throne of grace and ask you for your wisdom in exchange for my old ways of thinking and doing. I submit to you now and receive your peaceable, considerate, impartial, and sincere wisdom from above. Help me to be full of mercy so that I can bear good fruit for your Kingdom and live the life that you predestined for me, even before time began. In Jesus Christ's name, I pray. Amen and amen.

Now that we have taken the time to review and discuss the first step toward obtaining this key virtue called Humility, namely, reading and meditating on the Bible, you may be wondering, what is humility, and what can humility do for you? I believe the outcome of having a humble spirit will help you to embrace truth in your heart and unlock the next key principle (having a teachable spirit) to discover your identity in Christ, unlocking your God-given destiny and ultimately reclaiming your position in His Kingdom. Jesus said, "Blessed are the poor in spirit: for theirs is the kingdom of heaven…Blessed are the meek: for they shall inherit the earth" (Matt. 5:3,5). The end results will position you to become a successful servant of God's heart and live the purpose-filled life you've been searching for. You can begin living this life today. You can live it right here on Earth, as he predestined it in heaven long before time began. Are you ready? Let's GO!

My Story

The Birthing of a Warrior

"For I know the plans I have for you," declares the Lord, "plans to prosper you and not to harm you, plans to give you hope and a future.

— Jeremiah 29:11

I was born and raised in a little city called Pensacola, the westernmost town in the Florida Panhandle. The current population is approximately 52,713, showing growth since the last official Census taken in 2010. (worldpopulationreview.com/us-cities/pensacola-population). I am the oldest girl of seven children. My biological mother was young, had been married, but was divorced and single by the time I came along, leaving my grandmother and great-grandmother to help with raising her children.

By the time we children were school age, my young mother decided she wanted to move to New York City; however, my grandmother and great-grandmother refused to allow her to take us, girls, with her. She was told if she left, she could take the boys, but had to leave the girls behind with them because they were concerned for our safety and the possibility of us being taken advantage of. My mother was respectful and honored their request, and off to New York City, she went with my two older brothers. My grandmother and great-grandmother were already somewhat up in age, and life became even more challenging for them after assuming the great responsibility of raising my sisters and me; so much so that the school system got involved. At some point, the school system contacted Child Protective Services, which back in the day was referred to as the Welfare Department.

My sisters and I were attending AA Dixon Elementary School during this time. I don't believe I will ever forget that dreadful day when a Caucasian man and woman came to the school and hauled my sister and me off without any notice. Although they were smiling at us and appeared to be nice people, deep down within, I knew something was terribly wrong. Just recalling this has stirred up a deep, gut-wrenching pain. Who were these people? Where were my grandmother and great-grandmother? Did they know we were being taken away?

In my mind's eye, I can still see that big, black car they were driving. They told us they had come to take us for a ride in the big black car. But when we resisted, they scooped us up against our will as we screamed, cried, and kicked to no avail.

This apparently was prearranged by the school because the principal and teachers were standing there but did nothing to stop them. We were taken to a stranger's (lady) home who was waiting for us when we arrived. The white man and woman told us she is our foster mother, and she would be taking care of us. We were beyond sad. We were traumatized. Again, just recalling this event has brought tears to my eyes, and as I look back, perhaps this is where my warrior spirit began, hence the subtitle to my first book, *Simply Faith: The Birthing of a Warrior.*

Adopted

Praise God! He is faithful to His Word. He does have a plan, a purpose, and a God-given destiny for our lives. I want to interject right here and testify that I have never, ever, held anything against my dear biological mother, Jeannette Summers, who passed away at the tender age of 66 on February 12, 2006, a few months after retiring from serving in the Social Security Administration for over 20 years.

My auntie Celestine, my mother's sister, came to our rescue and fought to get my sisters and me back and out of the child protection system. She was instrumental in getting us placed in homes with people she knew. My sister Ginne and I ended up being adopted by Auntie Celestine's sister-in-law, Lottie, who has now gone on to be with the Lord. Mama Lottie was married to a man named James, but they never had any children together. Lottie had one son, Mack, who was much older than us girls. I never knew much about Mack's biological father, but the story was told that he was in the Marine Corps and was killed in action. However, Lottie always wanted to have a girl, and here was her chance to fulfill her dream. She received a double blessing; two girls instead of one!

Look at the faithfulness of our God, the Creator. He remembered Mama Lottie's desires, and His plan for our lives was fulfilled too. Pick up a copy of my first book, *Simply Faith: The Birthing of a Warrior*, for the complete story. Perhaps you may have a similar story or know someone who does.

The point I would like to make is that we must always remember that it was God, the Creator of the universe, who created everything in the fullness of His time, which includes you and me. See Colossians 2:15-17 NKJV. He knew from the very beginning that the trajectory of our lives would play out the way it has. You may be asking, but why? Why was I adopted? Why did my parents give me away? Why me? Why did this thing or that thing happen to me? Well, we must also remember that according to the Bible, God created the heavens and the Earth, and everything He created was good (Gen. 1:31) NKJV.

Man was created in the image and likeness of God. God created man to walk in close fellowship with him. However, when the first man, Adam, and his wife, Eve, disobeyed God, sin entered the world, and they lost their identity and oneness with God. They were no longer walking in union with him, and from this point forward, man has attempted to live independently of his Creator, God. So, this is the reason for the brokenness that we see all around us. The Problem: Pride. The man became puffed up with pride, desiring to run his own life without any regard to the plans and purposes of God. The entire human race was now born into sin with the same prideful spirit as Lucifer (the devil).

The Bible says, "There is a way *that seems* right to a man, but its end *is* the way of death" (Prov. 14:12). My mother chose to do her own thing. She decided to live her life independent of her mother and grandmother's advice but, more importantly, independent of God, her Creator. She was not the only one with the spirit of pride. Pride is a spiritual matter and is indeed rampant in all of us, which is why we all need a Savior.

The passage above that states, "…but its end is the way of death," this could be a physical or spiritual death, which means a separation from God. We all need Jesus (Rom. 3:23). And, thank God for his everlasting love and loving-kindness, which drew my mother back to him many years before she passed away. But Lucifer was cast down from heaven because of his pride and the revolt he led against God. He wanted to take God's place. He said in his heart that he would be like God. He wanted to be worshiped and exalted above God, the Creator. (Isa. 14:12–15). He lost his place and position with God forever!

But God had mercy on us, His creation. He made a way possible for us to be reunited with him. God didn't forget about the fragility of man, His creation. He knows our frame. He knows that we are but dust (Ps. 103:14).

The issue lies with us, mankind. We must remember that we can't do anything without God. It was He who breathed the breath of life in us, and we became a living being (Gen. 2:7). God is all-knowing. He made provision for us, even before we were born. God knew that my sisters and I would be adopted— long before the inception of an adoption agency, a Child Protective Service, or a Welfare Department, for that matter. He predestined us to adoption by His Son, Jesus Christ, to Himself, according to the good pleasure of His will, to the praise of the glory of His grace, by which He made us accepted in the Beloved. We have been redeemed (purchased back) through His blood, the forgiveness of sin, according to the riches of His grace (Eph. 1:5–7). King David said, "When my father and my mother forsake me, Then the Lord will take care of me" (Ps. 27:10).

❖ *Reflections*

The first step to obtaining the grace of God is to humble yourself and say, as Psalm 27:11 says, "Teach me Your way, O Lord, and lead me in a smooth path…" What is the next practical step you can take toward obtaining the grace of God in your life? No matter what situation you may find yourself in, know that the same God who adopted me and took me in as His own once again will do the same thing for you if you are willing to humble yourself and acknowledge him as Lord and Savior. Don't wait. Act today! See the Prayer of Salvation at the end of the book or simply pray out loud as the Apostle Paul taught us in his letter to the Romans, chapter 10, verse 9.

"I believe in my heart that Jesus is the Son of God, that he died for my sins, and God raised him from the dead."
You too can be ADOPTED in the Beloved!

Biblical Humility

He has told you, O man, what is good; And what does the Lord require of you Except to be just, and to love [and to diligently practice] kindness (compassion), And to walk humbly with your God [setting aside any overblown sense of importance or self-righteousness].

— Micah 6:8 (Amplified Bible)

Humility is the fear of the LORD; Its wages are riches and honor and life" (Prov. 22:4 New International Version). Did you catch that? The pay for humility is riches, honor, and life! And just to be clear, the fear mentioned in this verse is referring to the reverence of the LORD, not a fear that terrorizes, but a reverent one. The Amplified Bible states it this way: "The reward of humility *and* the reverent *and* worshipful fear of the Lord is riches and honor and life." So, what does humility mean? According to Webster (online Dictionary) "*Humility* is freedom

from pride or arrogance: the quality or state of being humble." And *humble* is defined as "not proud or haughty: not arrogant or assertive." As we can see in the Scripture above, *Humility* causes us to respond to the LORD in a *"reverent"* way, which means honor, or respect felt or shown: deference, especially: profound adoring awed respect." Humility causes us to acknowledge the Lord for who He is and to give honor to whom honor is due.

Sinful pride, on the other hand, is the opposite of humility, and it causes one to dishonor the Lord? This is the very sin that caused Lucifer (the devil) to fall from God's grace forever. I am so grateful to God for His loving-kindness, tender mercy, and patience with me through the years as I struggled with wanting to have my own way and feeling the need to look out for my own personal interests rather than the interests of others as the Scripture commands. We are to follow Christ as He is the perfect example of selfless humility.

In our relationships with one another, we are to have the same mindset as Christ. (Phil. 2: 1-5) NIV.

I began to realize that my so-called Christian conduct was lacking in humility in so many ways which, in fact, if truth be told, my conduct was dishonoring to the Lord. I know, I am not in this alone. Have you ever had an "overblown sense of importance or self-righteousness," as stated above in Mic. 6:8? If so, how did you handle it? Were you aware that your inactions were pride and were offensive to God? James 4:6; states, "… "God is opposed to the proud *and* haughty, but [continually] gives [the gift of] grace to the humble [who turn away from self-righteousness (AMP Bible).

Wow! But, look at what God gives to the humble. His grace. God will bestow upon us, His grace, mercy, and kindness which provides us with the ability (His divine strength) to exercise this Christian virtue called Humility. Why is this important to God? It's essential because it positions us to be a blessing to others, which brings glory and honor to God.

As we yield to His ways, the more our eyes are opened to see ourselves as He sees us, holy, beloved, and blameless, which is found in His Son, Jesus Christ, and Him alone. (Eph. 1:5; Col. 1:22) NIV. Because of this revelation, we are better equipped to foster positive relationships with others even amid our cultural, social, economic and spiritual differences; then we can live harmoniously and avoid the pitfalls of self-exaltation, jealousy, strife, and competition.

Having our eyes and hearts enlightened to who we are in God is a must if we are to begin the process of "unlocking our God-given destiny" which I believe is achieved by embracing what I propose to be the master key virtue called Humility.

According to the Scripture above, riches, honor, and life are the rewards for living a life of humility. What about your life right now? Are you experiencing riches, honor and the life that you were created to live? Do you have questions about why you were created? Would you like to know God's Plan for your life? Or do you think you know what's best for you? I want to encourage you right here. Whatever you do, don't allow your pride to get in the way and prevent you from unlocking the most beautiful and exciting life you could ever imagine. I believe God, knows what's best for me, you, and every person on the face of this Earth. Why, because after all, He is the Creator, and we are His workmanship. Eph. 2:10 (NKJV).

One practical step toward humility is to embrace all that God has done for us through His Son, Jesus Christ. By doing so, it will enable us to say "Yes" to God's plans and then He will begin to Sovereignly change our thinking, our motives, goals and desires and perhaps we will avoid the messy dilemma, the disciples found themselves in as they questioned Jesus.

The disciples of Jesus asked Him, "Who is the greatest in the Kingdom of heaven?" I am quite sure they were surprised by His action and answer. He called a little child to Himself and sat in the midst of them, and said, "Assuredly, I say to you unless you are converted and become as little children, you will by no means enter the kingdom of heaven." He went on to say, "Therefore, whoever **humbles** *emphasis mine* himself as this little child is the greatest in the kingdom of heaven" (Matt. 18:1–4 NKJV).

Now, are we saying to be humble, one must walk with his or her head down and think of themselves as being nothing or a nobody? Or, to be childish? Most certainly not! That thought is farthest away from the truth on what God thinks about humility and how we are to live it out. How could this be, if we are made in God's image, which, according to the Bible, we are. "Then God said, 'Let Us make man in Our Image, according to Our likeness…'"

"So, God created man in His *own* image; in the image of God, He created him; male and female He created them." (Gen. 1:26–27).

God expects His children to have child-like humility and a heart ready to not only serve but also to trust and depend on Him as their Source, rather than themselves and/or something that He has not established or ways that He has not directed. So, humility, or to humble oneself, is the opposite of pride. For the purpose of this book, when I speak of pride, I am referring to sinful pride, because the Bible speaks of two types of pride: one is good, and is based on a pride for others who are living in obedience to God (2 Cor. 7:1–4). An example of good pride is found in 2 Corinthians 5:12 (NIV): "We are not trying to commend ourselves to you again, but are giving you an opportunity to take pride in us, so that you can answer those who take pride in what is seen rather than in what is in the heart."

The second type is selfish pride, which is sinful. It can be defined as "*excessive* confidence or glorification in one's self, possessions, etc.," (Daily Bible Study, by Wayne Blank) and is associated with words like *haughtiness, arrogance,* and *conceit,* all of which are opposite of Godly humility. This type of pride leads to disobedience and destruction because it opposed God and was the first sin committed by Adam and Eve, which caused the entire human race to fall into temptation.

Going back to the fact that we all were created in the image of God, let's take a closer look at the words of exhortation from the Apostle Paul in the book of Philippians. He stated, "Let this mind be in you, which was in Christ, Jesus: Who…made Himself of no reputation, and took upon Him, the form of a servant and was made in the likeness of men. And being found in fashion as a man, He humbled Himself and became obedient unto death, even the death of the cross" Phil. 5-8 (KJV).

The Passion Translation reads, "Laying your life down in tender surrender before the Lord will bring life, prosperity, and honor as your reward" (Prov. 22:4). Wow! "Laying your life down in tender surrender…" You may be wondering, what is all of this tender surrender and how is one to live this humility thing out? Let's take a short trip back to the garden. You ask, the garden? What's in the garden? Yes, I believe we will discover a few clues in the Garden of Eden, where it all began. Are you ready to lay your life down in tender surrender before the Lord? If so, pray this simple prayer, based on Jer.10:23, "Lord, *please help me to surrender my life to you and live according to Your great plans. In Jesus, Name, I pray. Amen"*

❖ *Reflections*

Can you think of a time when you felt the need or the entitlement to exalt yourself above someone else? If so, what was that like? What was the outcome? How did you feel afterward?

Why do you suppose God is opposed to the proud and haughty (also referred to as high-mindedness). List one or two practical steps you can take to safeguard yourself against the sinful pride that God is opposed to.

The Garden of Eden

A man's pride will bring him low. Man fell from God's Grace. Why? Disobedience separated him from God. The Inception: The Garden of Eden The Solution: Humility. Humble yourselves in the sight of the Lord, and he will lift you up.

The late Dr. Myles Munroe is one of my heroes. I have a small library of his books and enjoy reading and gleaning from his writings. In his book *God's Big Idea, Reclaiming God's Original Purpose for Your Life,* he said, "Religion is man's idea, not God's. God's original idea is much bigger and much better than anything we humans could ever dream up." He said it was God's idea to "extend his heavenly Kingdom to the earthly plane, to expand his supernatural realm into the natural.… God decided to fill the Earth with the culture of heaven." He goes on to say, "When God decided to bring the culture of heaven to Earth, he did not use war. He did not use conquest. He did not issue a code of laws. No, when God set out to bring heaven to Earth, he did something much simpler; something uniquely beautiful and wonderful."

So, what did God do? God planted a garden. The Garden of Eden. We pick this story up in Genesis 2:8–9,15–16 (NKJV). "The Lord God planted a garden eastward in Eden, and there He put the man whom He had formed. And out of the ground, the Lord God made every tree grow that is pleasant to the sight and good for food. The tree of life *was* also in the midst of the garden, and the tree of the knowledge of good and evil. Then the Lord God took the man and put him in the garden of Eden to tend and keep it. And the Lord God commanded the man, saying, "Of every tree of the garden you may freely eat; but of the tree of the knowledge of good and evil you shall not eat, for in the day that you eat of it you shall surely die."

Did you see that? The Lord God planted a garden! I am always amazed when I read God planted a garden. How incredible is that? The One True God, Elohim, the Creator of the universe, planted a garden for man. That should be a reminder of how much he loves us and desires to have fellowship with his children. God did not hire someone to do this on His behalf. No, He did it Himself!

So now, what exactly happened in this garden? Plain and simple, man disobeyed God. From what I can tell, Adam and Eve had free access to everything in that garden to eat, except for that one command, "Do not eat from the tree of the knowledge of good and evil." (Gen 2:17) NIV. There were going to be consequences if Adam ate from that tree, and so it was just as God said it would be. In Genesis Chapter 3, we see the temptation and the fall of man. Lucifer (the devil) beguiled Eve by telling her a lie.

It appears Eve may have gotten the message a little twisted when she added to the command, "You shall not touch it." (Gen. 3:3) NIV. God did not say anything about touching the tree, but He did say if they ate of it, death would surely come.

Eve's first mistake was talking to the devil. The Bible calls him the "father of lies" (Jn. 8:44). He was a rebel, and no longer a part of God's Kingdom. What did he know? Nothing but lies! He lied to her when he said,

"You will not surely die. For God knows that in the day you eat of it, your eyes will be opened, and you will be like God, knowing good and evil." (Gen. 3:4-5) NIV.

Stop and ask yourself, are you being lied to? What is that devil saying to you? Remember, he can't tell the truth, even if he wants to! Now, we see in Genesis 1:26, the TRUTH is Eve, and Adam was ALREADY like God. They were created in His image, after His own likeness. How could they not be like Him? God loved them so much that, just like us, He gave them their own free will. God desires that we choose to obey Him willingly, not out of terror, but out of love.

God cannot lie. He will NOT tolerate sin. Disobedience is sin in its purest form. Are you willing to trust and obey God? Look what happened to Eve and her husband as a result of following the lie of the devil. She saw that the tree was good for food, pleasant to the eyes, and a tree desirable to make one wise. This is the perfect setup for the pride of life. I am sure she thought to herself, *What's in it for me? Hmmm! Let me see. Maybe that devil has a point?*

So, what did she do? She took of the fruit and ate, and gave it to Adam, her husband. And their eyes were opened. They knew they were naked and felt shame; and, thus, covered themselves with fig leaves (Gen. 3:6–7). Did you catch that? They covered themselves. Here is attempt number one at their independence from God, their Maker. I can't count how many times I have failed at trying to do things on my own, excluding God, and only later making a total fool of myself and then came crawling back, asking God to please help me. I know that I am not in this alone. I am sure we have all done this at one time or another. What about you? Can you think of a time when you've done this too? And, if so, what was the outcome?

But, here, we see God in His mercy at work again. The Bible says, "He made tunics of skin and covered them" (verse 21). Up until the time they disobeyed God, they were enjoying their close fellowship with Him. Perhaps walking and talking with Him in the cool of the garden. Now, they had lost their identity. They were no longer like God. This was not His best for them. And neither is it His best for you and me.

God knew the plans and purpose for which He had created His first family from the beginning. God had blessed them. He said to them, "Be fruitful and multiply. Fill the earth and subdue it. Have dominion over the fish of the sea, over the birds of the air, and over every living thing that moves on the earth..." (Gen. 1:28–30).

Adam and Eve were in their kingly position, living their lives full of purpose. But sadly, God had to expel them from the Garden of Eden, just like He had to expel Lucifer from heaven. Why? All because of prideful sin. They lost their identity and kingly position because of disobedience.

But I am here to encourage you that God, in His mercy and grace, did not leave us without hope! He had a plan of redemption all along. Dr. Myles Munroe states, "The Bible is about the rise, fall, and rise of God's Kingdom on Earth. It tells the story of a kingdom established, a kingdom lost, and a kingdom regained." He further states: "Heaven is God's first and original Kingdom. As a kingdom with God as its King. Heaven is a country just as real as any nation on Earth, even though invisible." God rules His Kingdom by divine right, by right of creation. Because God created all things, all things belong to Him. He alone is the rightful ruler of the universe" (Ps. 103:19).

Yes, God desired to expand His Kingdom from heaven to Earth. He did so by creating mankind and giving him dominion to rule over the Earth, but as Dr. Myles Munroe stated, "He never gave us ownership. God is King of the Earth, and Adam and Eve were its stewards, imbued with almost unlimited authority to rule in his name."

Even King David was amazed at what the God of the universe thought of His creation. He said, "When I consider Your heavens, the work of Your fingers, the moon and the stars, which You ordained, what is man that You are mindful of him, and the son of man that You visited him? For You have made him a little lower than the angels, and You have crowned him with glory and honor. You have made him to have dominion over the works of Your hands; You have put all things under his feet, all sheep and oxen—even the beasts of the field, the birds of the air, and the fish of the sea that pass through the paths of the seas" (Ps. 8:3–8).

You see, God has perfect knowledge of man. He made us. He saw us before we were born and scheduled each day of our life before we took one breath! And every day of our life has been recorded in His book. Did you know that His thoughts toward us are precious and that He is always thinking about you and me? King David said, "I can't even count how many times a day your thoughts turn toward me. And when I awaken in the morning, you are still thinking of me!" (Ps. 139:16–18). Wow! I have goosebumps just reading this all over again.

I say we must get back to Eden, the King's way of living. However, we can't do it independently of God, the King. You may be asking; how do I get back to the King's way of living? No matter what man may think or theorize, it is clear that "...we are His workmanship, created in Christ Jesus for good works, which God prepared beforehand that we should walk in them" (Eph. 2:10).

Now, if this is so—and it is—then Jesus is the ONLY way back to the King's way of living. It's plain and simple. Jesus himself said, "I am the way, the truth, and the life. No one comes to the Father except through Me" (Jn. 14:6). Do you want to get back to the King's way of living? I pray your answer is YES! And YES again! Because the Father, God, wants to restore YOU back to YOUR rightful, kingly position! *"Humble yourselves in the sight of the Lord, and he will lift you up!" (Jas. 4:10) NKJV*

Pray this simple prayer based on Jer. 33:3 "Lord, I call upon Your name, and I know that you will hear me and answer me. I ask that you teach me how to humble myself in your sight." In Jesus, Name, I pray. Amen.

❖ *Reflections*

Do you know that you were created in the image of God, and He gave you dominion over the work of His hands? What are your thoughts on this biblical truth? What one step could you take now to start moving toward the King's way of living?

A Test Of Humility: Funny Story

Humility will open more doors than arrogance ever will.

— Zig Ziglar

Here's a funny story. I was reminded of a time back in 1989, when, during a church service, a young lady by the name of Barbara politely tapped me on my shoulder and said, "The Lord told me to give this to you." Now, mind you, she and I had no relationship other than Hello, Sister. She handed me a tiny piece of paper that was folded and had been ripped out from a small memo tablet. I unfolded the paper and noted, "Proverbs 3:5–6." There was no explanation and nothing else written other than this reference to the passage of Scripture. I politely smiled, thanked her, and pretended that I knew exactly what the Scripture was about. Talk about humility! Some humility that was. Isn't that how we do it when we want to make a good impression on others, especially our Church family? What she did not know, however, was that I had just stepped into an Interim Acting Director of Nursing position (1½ years after moving to Hawaii) that I and everyone else at that hospital knew I was not qualified for. It was a "God Move," and no one, nowhere, could change it. Not even me. I was a young nurse, about twenty-eight years old, and I had no desire to oversee anyone. I was perfectly content with taking care of patients as a floor nurse and escorting patients back and forth from our hospital via ambulance to the largest hospital on the island, which was a trauma center where they had the diagnostic equipment necessary for specialized procedures/testing.

I was asked several times to accompany a few patients from our island back to their neighboring islands. There was a nursing shortage back in those days, and hospital management needed whoever, and whoever would say yes to help fill the gaps for these odd tasks/requests that periodically came up, and often at the most inconvenient times ever. I was just happy to serve wherever there was a need, as long as it didn't require me to do too much talking, especially since it seemed the majority of the people (nurses, patients, and other hospital personnel) seemed to be speaking their native language versus plain-old, simple English.

I was also having a challenging time pronouncing their names. So, for me, there was a perceived language barrier, in most cases. It wasn't unusual for me to spell the doctor's name when calling the hospital operator to page him or her, all because I could NOT pronounce the name! It became an inside joke for the operators and me. They came to know me rather quickly and would tease me (in a polite way) whenever they saw me in person.

My personality was more of an introvert, and it was natural for me to work/hide behind the scenes whenever possible. So, it was easy for me to do the odd jobs, just show up, deliver the patient, hand the medical staff the folder that contained the patient's medical information. Boom! Mission accomplished! I was off the hook and on to the next simple task. My nursing colleagues thought I was a little strange for volunteering for these tasks. However, I felt it released me from having to struggle with the language barrier, and it was a safety net.

Fast-forward; little did I know, God had other plans in store for me.

Side note: I tell the story in my first book, *Simply Faith: The Birthing of a Warrior* of how I always dreamed of living in Hawaii, even as a young child.

Now, back to the story. So, here I am, finally in my dream place—Hawaii, the desire of my heart—and scared out of my wits because I literally was "put" in this new position. You may be wondering, how did I end up in this job? Glad you asked! One day, I received a phone call from Mrs. B., the hospital administrator secretary. She said, "Shelia, Mr. M— would like to see you in his office tomorrow morning; can you make it?"

Now, what was I to say? No, I am sorry I am not available and can't make it? Of course not! I mustered up the energy with a response, "Sure, I can be there.

What time?" We confirmed the appointment, and the call ended. I was totally miserable throughout the rest of the evening and night before. I couldn't sleep, tossing and turning in bed all night long, wondering what Mr. M— could possibly want to see me about.

Daylight came all too soon, and it was time for the meeting. I had never been summoned to the hospital administrator's office before, and the truth is, I was shaking like a leaf on a tree when I went into the meeting and when I came out of the meeting. I don't recall if smoking in the hospital back in the day was permitted or not. However, I do remember Mr. M— sitting in his BIG office at his BIG desk in his BIG swivel chair and had a BIG pipe in a glass-like ashtray on his desk. He was a rather BIG man, very professional, but had a BOOMING voice that commanded one's attention. Long story short, I could not believe my ears. He got right to the matter and said he had heard good things about me and went on to say that by law, he would need to name an interim director of nursing (DON) for the long-term care facility within one week. The current DON had submitted her resignation unexpectedly and was unable to provide the appropriate notice due to unforeseen circumstances. (Testimony for my next book in this series.)

He then asked me if I would consider taking this position on. I was in total shock! My entire body became weak and limp. It felt like the blood rushed from my brain and went straight into my stomach. I thought I was going to faint right there in front of him. I managed to compose myself, and before I could say anything, he interrupted and said, "Oh, you can think about it and let me know your decision by tomorrow." Whew! What a relief, so I thought.

I stumbled out of that office and made my way to my car. I remember crying all the way home that afternoon after work, thinking to myself, *what in the world will I do?* I couldn't think fast enough. My mind was racing like a speed car. I knew that I didn't want to say yes, but then, I thought if I said no, he would probably fire me, and I wouldn't have a job at all. I felt trapped!

I believe the Lord has a sense of humor because when I arrived home and told my husband (at the time), I thought he would understand the dilemma that I faced and would empathize with me. Well, that did not happen. He politely reminded me of how I used to come home and talk to him about how much I loved the elderly people and wished I had a big home to put them in and take care of them all. I had forgotten about that. And then the Holy Spirit gently reminded me of a song, "Lord, Here I am, Send Me" that I used to sing just about every morning as I drove out the back gate of Hickam AFB, going to work at the hospital. I remember, as if it was yesterday, I came back with, "Yes, but I didn't say I wanted fifty-five of them!" As mentioned earlier, I was content running around performing odd jobs/tasks that I felt comfortable with.

By this time, I had been a nurse for almost nine years. I'd spent the first seven years working at a large hospital in my hometown Pensacola. So, it's not like I didn't have any experience. But as I think back, my indecision was more out of fear. It's funny because I remember even back then when I was in Pensacola, and it was my turn to be the charge nurse on my floor, I always tried to find a way to bypass my turn and pass it on to one of the other young nurses who seemed eager and excited to take the charge position.

BUT GOD! He had a plan for my life, just as He does for your life if we only start to trust and believe that He knows what's best for us. He desires that we humble ourselves and acknowledge Him as the Lord over our lives, because, after all, He is the one who created us!

I am excited to tell you that God knew exactly how my life was going to turn out. He knew that if I accepted his invitation to join Him in his work, my life would never be the same again. I had a lot to learn, and totally admit that humility was nowhere on my radar as one of the virtues needed for where I was headed. That passage from Proverbs 3:5–6 became my lifeline. I did everything I could do to memorize those few verses. I wrote it on a yellow Post-it and taped it to the Rolodex that was on my BIG desk (that I was afraid to sit at.) And each morning that I came into my

BIG office, I would stand in front of the sink and run my hands under the warm water to settle my nerves and recite: "Trust in the Lord with all of your heart and lean not on your own understanding, in all your ways, acknowledge Him, and He shall direct your paths." The warmth of that water running on my hands and the words of that Scripture seemed to calm me.

That became my safe place when things got tough out there on the nursing floor. I would run to my office, lock the door, and retreat until I gathered up the nerve to go out there again. I did not consider myself to be humble by accepting the small, odd task that others thought was beneath them to do because we were nurses. And, looking back, I am glad that I did not know that I was humble, because had I known, I am sure it would have turned into puffed-up pride, the very opposite of humility. These small tasks led to the bigger doors opening (which, by the way, was part of my God-given destiny).

But God knew. And He knew that I needed Him. I was clueless about the significance of the task that was set before me. I had NO idea what it meant to be a director of nurses. I could not even pronounce the names of my staff, let alone understand what half of them were saying because of the language barrier. I was given the responsibility to run this 55-bed facility, which was an extension of the acute care hospital and a 24/7 operation, which included three shifts of nurses. The facility also had other departments (rehabilitation, activities, dietary, social services, and housekeeping), and I was responsible for overseeing the entire operation and providing educational/training of the long-term care state and federal regulatory requirements for the facility staff. Talk about needing God's help and His grace and mercy! This needs to be a movie someday!

I need to take a praise break right here and say, BUT GOD! He never left me, and He never failed me. God was right there through every experience, through the laughter and tears—and believe me, there were times of many tears. He guided me through every situation that came up, and today, I can say it was one of the greatest highlights of my life experiences.

I could not see this during the process. There were many days and nights that I wanted to give up. I could not figure this out; who signed me up for this? I began to question myself as the others were questioning me—and they queried me for years. "How did you get that job, Shelia?" they would ask repeatedly. But God had positioned me right in the middle of His will and plans for my life.

I was growing in every area of my life: spiritually, personally, socially, professionally, as well as financially. He favored my life in more ways than I can count. My salary increased overnight, so much so that I could not keep up with the amount of money that I was making (which, a few years later became a problem, as I started to turn my attention more and more toward material things; another story for another book).

But, thank God for His loving-kindness and patience as He helped me take my eyes off the things of the world (the pride of life) and refocus on what mattered most, which was to seek first the kingdom of God and His righteousness and then everything else would be added (Matt. 6:33). He is Jehovah Jireh, the Lord God who provides. He continues to amaze me in all that He is doing in my life as I am still learning to depend on Him to lead and guide me in the way in which I should go.

God had prepared this work for me to do before time began (Eph. 2:10) and, of course, for a higher purpose, something bigger than myself. God knew that one day in the fullness of time (on His timetable), I would step into my destiny and purpose, which is to open up Zoe The God-Kind of Life Healing Home right here in my Island State, the state that God called me to. I am blessed to be a blessing, just as He promised Abraham that all families in the earth through him would be blessed (Gen. 12:1–3). Another testimony for the second book in this series. Look out, world, cause here I come! To God, be the glory for the things He has done!

❖ *Reflections*

Be brave. Be bold. Humble yourself and ask God what work did he give you to do? Imagine you are walking in your God-given destiny now. Envision it in specific details. What do you see, and what emotions are you sensing?   What is one thing you can do today to move you closer to your God-given destiny?

Humility: Dying To Self

For the LORD has called you
Like a woman forsaken and grieved in spirit,
Like a youthful wife when you were refused,"
Says your God.
"For a mere moment I have forsaken you,
But with great mercies, I will gather you.
With a little wrath, I hid My face from you for a
moment;
But with everlasting kindness, I will have mercy on
you,"
Says the LORD, your Redeemer.

— Isaiah 54:6–8 (NKJV)

God is gracious! As I sit here once again pondering on how to begin this chapter, I remember as if it was yesterday the days and months that led up to September 24, 2004, the day my ex-husband moved out. I never thought I would be writing a book about humility, and especially one that involves the intimate details of my personal affairs as I literally fought to live physically and spiritually. However, I am a living witness that God (Jehovah Rapha) is a Healer and a Deliverer. I guess you don't know what you don't know until you come face-to-face with reality.

My spiritual mother, Imelda, was a great mentor, teacher, and an exhorter for one to get to know Jesus for themselves. She would say. "Babies"—referring to the young ladies in the Bible study— "you all need to know Jesus and not only in the power of His resurrection, but also in the fellowship of His suffering" (Phil. 3:10–11). She would say, "You all are very good at testifying and saying, 'I want to know Him in the power of His resurrection,' but you all stop right there." She would ask, "What about His suffering?"

Wow! You could hear a pin drop in the room. I know for sure; I didn't know anything about His suffering and wasn't so sure I wanted to find out. At that point in my life, things were going well. I was happy, satisfied, and comfortable. Nothing to complain about, hence the reason I wasn't interested in learning about His suffering. Seriously, life was good at that time.

As I researched this topic on humility in preparation to write my book, I came across this article online that I feel addresses and answers the questions that I had during one of many encounters I had with the Lord after my ex-husband moved out and the seemingly endless agony and suffering. Here's a portion of that article, and I will share my testimony at the end of it. The author stated, "Just as Jesus 'bore our griefs and carried our sorrows' (Isa. 53:4), so we are to *participate in his suffering*—by barring ourselves from sin and self, and choosing instead to follow what he would have us do (Rom. 8:17)." He goes on to say, "'Suffering' simply means *barring ourselves* (or preventing ourselves) *from following sin and self. (*1 Pet. 4:19)." This is what Phil. 3:10 refers to when it says, "That I may know Him, and the power of His resurrection, and the *fellowship of His sufferings* being made conformable unto His death." He states, "We are to identify with Christ, not only by verbally

assenting to, ascribing to and holding on to what He did for us on the cross, but also by daily experiencing the crucifying of our own 'self.' In other words, we are to bear our own cross and follow Jesus. (Matt. 16:24)."
Wow! This says it all.

Testimony: Dying To Self

And he said to all, "If anyone would come after me,
let him deny himself and take up his cross daily and
follow me."

— Luke 9:23

I had been perfectly healthy up until this time. I worked out five days a week at the gym, (bodybuilding) inspired by one of the female ushers at my church; training for my third upcoming Honolulu Marathon, for which I ran long distances every Saturday; worked a full-time, on-call, 24/7 job at a large hospital; attended church practically every Sunday and facilitated the Women's Bible Study every Tuesday evening. Looking from the outside, I was super fit. Seriously! I had finally accomplished my goal—those Angela Bassett biceps—and had done crunches and sit-ups and forsaken ALL sodas, just to obtain the famous six-pack abs that every woman yearns for!

However, amid all of this, there I was, suffering in silence as I was preparing for my ex-husband to move out. I will never forget the date because it was a special day for the women of the chapel; Sunday, September 19, 2004, Protestant Women of the Chapel (PWOC) Sunday. It was our Sunday to lead the worship service, and I was asked to read the announcements. I remember turning around and asking the chaplain if I could share a testimony before reading them, to which he consented.

I shared my testimony (which had nothing to do with what I was going through at the time) and proceeded to read. As I turned around to leave the pulpit area, I stumbled as I walked back to my pew. I thought I had tripped over my shoe. However, as soon as I sat down, it seemed as if someone pulled a black curtain over my eyes. I felt lightheaded and turned to the young lady sitting next to me and asked if she had something to drink because I felt like my blood sugar was low. Back in those days, I was strict with my diet, and if I didn't have access to food that fueled my body, I would rather skip a meal and eat later than eat something unhealthy.

The young lady didn't have anything other than the juice that was in her baby bottle, which I quickly gulped down to avoid fainting. Wow! What memories. Oh, the smell of sour milk from that bottle!

Long story short, this was the beginning of an almost three-year battle with dizzy spells that led to months of doctor and ER visits and thank God only two hospital admissions. Oddly enough, the medical professionals could not find the cause of the dizzy spells and wanted to treat me for all kinds of things—depression, low blood pressure, and low blood sugar—which I declined because I was determined to extinguish the fiery darts of the enemy.

Looking back, I did suffer some of the strikes from the fiery darts of the enemy. However, I had more than likely given him access and became an easy target. How? You may ask. Pride. I am sure I was full of it from day one when I decided that I didn't need anyone. I didn't tell my boss; no one knew that my world had been turned upside down. However, because I worked at the hospital, and my personal doctor was also the employee physician, she made sure that I had an extensive workup, which meant that I was seen practically by every specialist there was, from cardiology to endocrinology to neurology to ENT; and of course, the gynecologist for hormone testing.

Long story short again—nothing, absolutely nothing. "You are the picture of health. We don't know what's wrong with you," the cardiologist told me. However, he wanted to perform the "Bubble test" to check if I had a hole in my heart (patent foramen ovale if you're going to get technical), which could cause the blood to leak from the right side of my heart to the left side and possibly contribute to the near fainting episodes.

I finally agreed to have the "Bubble Test" and ran over to the cardiac department on my lunch break with the plan of returning to work. Well, to my surprise, I ended up in the hospital with what is called a TIA (Transient Ischemic Attack). My entire left side was weak. I had to be hospitalized overnight. I begged the nurse on the night shift to allow me to get up and attempt to walk by myself, to which she consented. Glory to God, although I was weak, I managed to walk without help as she walked behind me with the wheelchair.

On the next day, I pleaded with the doctors to let me go home, I needed to get back home to my prayer closet. (which was my downstairs bathroom!) I would sit in there it seemed for hours reading and meditating on Scriptures that spoke about why Jesus came to this earth. He came to heal the brokenhearted, to proclaim freedom to those who were captives, to open the eyes of the blind (both natural and spiritual blindness.) Lk. 4:18 (NJKV). I was that person. I needed healing in every area of my life. I had heard many testimonies of how Jesus had healed the sick; now, it was my turn to do my part, which was to search the Scriptures on healing for myself.

The word of God was my life, it was health to my flesh. It was my medicine. (Prov. 4:20-22). I read that it was impossible to please God without faith. And that

He was a rewarder of those who diligently seek after Him (Heb.11: 6) NJKV. I was desperate for Him. He was my Comforter. My prayer life and faith increased tremendously during this experience. The prayer closet is where I found the strength and willpower to "keep going" and "not give up!" When I say, it was a fight; it was a fight! There is **VICTORY** in the Prayer Closet. Later one Saturday morning, as I was mopping my floor upstairs outside the bathroom area, I had a vision (did not know that's what it was at the time). I was listening to my worship music, singing, and praying, and as usual, asking the Holy Spirit to please show me the source of the dizzy spells. I remember crying out to God and saying, "You made me, and I know you know all about me. What is wrong with me?" And lo and behold! It was sudden—it was as if I could see Jesus Christ on the cross (at first the sight was a little blurry), but the more I looked, the more precise the picture became and then I could see Him, stretched out wide on the cross, and I could see the nails in His hands (that is where my focus was), and I could see the blood trickling down His head and face.

And then it was as if I heard Him say, *"Shelia, you have to pick up your cross. Shelia, you have to carry your cross."* WOW!

And, BOOM, the vision was over as quickly as it came; it left. However, I remember falling to the floor, balling up in a fetal position, sobbing like a baby, and praying in the Spirit. I had mixed feelings. I was rejoicing and thanking God for showing me yet breaking at the same time. Strange to say, but I was also relieved, although I did not fully understand the meaning of it all. Nevertheless, the one thing that I knew, for sure, is that God had spoken, which gave me great peace.

The Holy Spirit impressed upon me during this time to read Psalm 119:73 "With your very own hands you formed me; now breathe your wisdom over me so I can understand you." I remember reading this verse numerous times and crying like a baby because I had a personal encounter with the Living God. He showed me through the vision and His written Word that He is God, He loves me, and He is with me.

Nonetheless, I had to make a choice—to deny my flesh, "die to self," swallow my prideful, sinful attitude, pick up my cross and carry it! I did not realize that I was full of pride, and it was holding me back from receiving the help that I needed. I always felt like I needed to be independent and do things on my own, partly because of how I was raised. I watched Mama Lottie (my adoptive mother) struggle for years after Uncle James (my adoptive father) passed away. She was a young widow, now with two young girls to raise—my sister and me—and she couldn't get any financial assistance; no welfare, no free food (commodity food; now food stamps) from any government program. It was years later before one brave life insurance agent from the Wilson Insurance company stepped in and fought (wrote letters to the Senate) on behalf of my mother to help her collect Uncle James' widows and children's Social Security benefit. So, for me, I thought it was the norm to "struggle" in silence because Mama Lottie sure had her share.

I read this passage of Scripture (Ps. 119:73–80) again and again in every Bible translation I could find and finally settled on the Message Bible because of its conversational style that I could understand. See the entire passage below for the context and meaning.

> With your very own hands, you formed me; now breathe your wisdom over me so I can understand you. When they see me waiting, expecting your Word, those who fear you will take heart and be glad. I can see now, God, that your decisions are right; your testing has taught me what's true and right. Oh, love me—and right now! —hold me tight! just the way you promised. Now comfort me so I can live, really live; your revelation is the tune I dance to.
>
> Let the fast-talking tricksters be exposed as frauds; they tried to sell me a bill of goods, but I kept my mind fixed on your counsel. Let those who fear you turn to me for evidence of your wise guidance. And let me live whole

and holy, soul and body, so I can always walk with my head held high.

So, my friend, if you want to unlock your God-given destiny and walk in the fullness of your purpose, then there's only one way, and it is His way. You must learn to pick up your cross and die to self to embrace the plans and purpose for which He created for you before time began. You may be asking, Shelia, how do I do that? The answer is, swallow your pride and acknowledge that you need Him, and then surrender your life to Him. If you're like me, I promise you; you will never regret it!

Prayer of Salvation (to be said out loud):

Dear Lord, I declare with my mouth that Jesus is Lord and believe in my heart that God raised Him from the dead, and I thank you that I am now saved. In Jesus, Name. Amen

❖ *Reflections*

What are some areas in your life where pride may be operating? Describe a situation where pride could hinder God's plans and purpose for your life. What resources do you need? Are you willing to swallow your pride and seek help?

Humility: Prayer

Pride is the problem; humility is the answer.

— Joyce Meyer

In the online article from "Got Questions: Your Questions Bible Answers," the author stated, "Humility increases when we are willing to be humbled by God, circumstances, and others. Our sinful natures do not want to be humbled. We tend to protect our pride as though it were our best friend, but pride gets in the way of our relationship with God."

The Bible is clear about what God thinks about pride. The Apostle James says God "resists the prideful but gives more grace to the humble" (Jas. 4:6) and in this same passage, we see that we have a role to play, which is, "humbling ourselves in the sight of the Lord," and then God will do his part in "lifting us up" (verse 10).

As I mentioned several times before, September 24, 2004, is the day my ex-husband moved out. We had been preparing for this day for approximately eight months. Yes, I did say preparing, because after I got over the shock of the fact that the divorce was inevitable, my only recourse was to go into survival mode. Again, it was a personal situation that I didn't tell a soul, not one person—not even my sister. I made plenty of excuses when my family asked about my ex-husband or ask to speak with him. He did not want to be exposed, so I covered for him by offering excuses as to why he was not around or able to come to the telephone whenever someone called to speak with him. I must admit, it didn't take Mama Lottie too long to figure out something wasn't quite right with my responses.

My ex-husband and I were very civil toward one another during this time, as he had decided it would be best that we start the weaning process before his actual move-out date (meaning, he began to disengage from certain activities that we usually did together, like running or working out; washing the cars after we ran on Saturdays; shopping together; eating together, etc.). It was his belief that doing so would help minimize the pain of the upcoming divorce.

Now, of course, I did not like this idea, but I pretty much had no choice but to agree with it. I tried everything imaginable to get my ex-husband to see that his suggestion was selfish and that he was thinking only of himself. Well, all my whining and crying did not work! It was to no avail. Looking back, I can see now where my motive was impure, but I never thought that it was due to *my* pride and not his. I was very good at pointing out how selfish I felt he was in even asking for a divorce that he and I both know (even to this day) was not warranted and had no biblical basis. But, again, hindsight is a master teacher. God, in His loving, merciful kindness, was right there amidst both of us, desiring to lavish His love and grace to sustain us as we went through this painful process, and all He required of me was but to humble myself. It was a refining process, and I was kicking hard against the inevitable. See my testimony below.

TESTIMONY

Oh, my! I must pause and say that I did not expect to feel any emotions—some kind of way, as the saying goes—since it's been a little over 15 years that my ex-husband walked out the door. However, my heart just went *pitter-patter*, and I felt a bit of pain and sadness as those thoughts came crashing in like a wave upon my mind and heart. Geesh!

The time had come. My ex-husband had made several trips back and forth from our house to his new apartment to unload the boxes that I helped him pack. For some reason, I felt sorry for him and wanted to help any way that I could. So, there I was, now in the kitchen trying to pack dishes for him. The funny thing is that men are not concerned with how pretty the dishes are or if there are matching sets. Ladies, you know how we are; this kind of thing is important to us. So, there I was in the kitchen, making sure that he had a set of dishes that matched, as well as his favorite cooking utensils, pots, pans, and the famous wok that he loved using for stir-fry dishes. He loved to cook, at least when it came to Creole (Louisiana) style food!

Soon After, the packing was over, and he was finally on his way out the door as I sat on the stairwell watching him walk out that door for the last time as my husband. I had done well (so I thought) choking back the tears for days upon days, knowing that my crying was in vain, to the point where I said, "I have no more tears to cry." Well, at least that's what I thought.

Now, I had been pretty calm and accommodating with making sure we divided the furniture, linens, dishes, whatever was necessary; it was perfectly fine with me since we had accumulated these things over the nearly 25 years of marriage; it was no big deal to me. Material things were the least of my worries at that time. My health was on the line, as I was dealing with the sudden onset of dizzy spells, and now preparing to be left alone with no support in the house.

During the process of packing, I discovered he had forgotten the mink blankets one of his military buddies bring back from Korea for us. So, of course, I wanted to make sure he took his blanket with him and decided to remind him. Then, to my surprise, he turned around and said: "Those are my mink blankets. I paid for them. I am taking them both." WOW! I am not sure if it was the fact that he said he was taking them both or if it was the days and days of bottled-up tears stored up on the inside of me, but I lost it! I burst out sobbing like a baby as I sat on the stairwell, and it felt like my heart shattered in pieces.

Looking back, I probably had all kinds of pent-up anger, bitterness, pain, and the sting of rejection, you name it. And yes, he took both mink blankets! My tears did not dissuade him, not one bit! I remember crying so hard and for so long until my nose was clogged up, and I could not breathe. I was panting for air like a puppy, just to catch my breath. He walked out the door. And there I was now, all alone (and then I heard in my ear, those dreadful words—you are all alone now).

During this time, I was also having symptoms of low blood sugar, and as a nurse, I knew this could be dangerous. As I sat there on the stairwell crying until my eyes were almost swollen shut and a stuffy nose, I could hear that voice (the voice of the enemy) saying,

"See, you are all alone, and when you go to sleep, if your blood sugar drops, no one will know about it, and no one will be here to help you." Wow! Just reflecting on this time is literally giving me a headache. Someone, please help me say BUT GOD!

Not a single person will ever be able to tell me that God, Jesus Christ, and the Holy Spirit is not real. Just as quickly as I heard the enemy speaking to me in one ear, I could also hear the Holy Spirit speaking to me in my other ear, *"I will NEVER leave you, NOR forsake you."*

As Apostle Paul stated, "…Whether I was in my body or out of my body, I don't know—only God knows…" (2 Cor. 12:2).

All I know is that I heard the voice of the Holy Spirit, loud and clear. He then said in that still, small voice (in my spirit), *"Get up, go wash your face, and go to sleep."* I assure you; it was as if He was sitting right next to me and directing my next steps. I remember standing up and drying my face as I walked over to the closet. I grabbed a clean washcloth, washed my face, and got ready for bed.

Now, mind you, I had NEVER slept in a house overnight alone; and here I was, the first night (of many more to come) that I would be all alone. I was afraid to go to sleep before the Holy Spirit spoke to me because I had also heard the voice of the accuser (the devil, the enemy) who only speaks lies, for he can never tell the truth (Rev. 12:10; Jn. 8:44).

I don't recall when I fell off to sleep that night. I remember waking up to the sunlight shining in my bedroom window. I was shocked when I opened my eyes and realized that I was still lying in my bed, and no one had broken into my home to get me. Oh, so sad, but so true. The Holy Spirit is a Comforter, a Teacher, a Counselor, one who comes alongside to help us in our time of need. The Holy Spirit had to literally teach me how to go to sleep each night and to trust that He was there watching over me, and I had no reason to fear because He would never leave me nor forsake me. (More testimony for the next book).

I don't remember how many days and weeks passed. However, I vividly recall going back and forth to the doctor at least one to two times a week because of the dizzy spells. I thought I was a person of prayer before my world came crashing down (divorce, dizzy spells, etc.). But, little did I know a more profound connection was waiting on the other end of this chaos that I found myself in. I remember purchasing just about every cassette tape (yes, back then—cassette tapes indeed) on healing I could find. Every book, Bible, anything that spoke of God's healing power, I needed, and I pursued it. And let me put praise in for Christian television. Thank God for Trinity Broadcasting Network and Day Star Television stations. I watched Kenneth Copeland, Benny Hinn, Creflo Dollar, and Frederick Price Sr., just to name a few, on the healing and faith messages.

I will never forget Billy Brim was a guest on Kenneth Copeland Believers *Voice of Victory Broadcast* for a week, and of course, their messages are always centered on faith through the word of God. And healing was just a small thing for God because Jesus had already accomplished this for us through the cross. By this time, to be honest, I could not understand what was taking my healing so long to manifest; after all, I thought, I have done all I know to do. Well, I got a revelation one day, it seemed it was weeks after I had heard Billy Brim say on that program, "God is light, and in him, there is no darkness" (1 Jn. 1:5).

When I don't understand something, I typically will do my own research of the Scriptures, as Paul encouraged the saints to do. "Now the Berean Jews were of more noble character than those in Thessalonica, for they received the message with great eagerness and examined the Scriptures every day to see if what Paul said was true" (Acts 17:11 NIV).

So, where am I going with this, and what does this have to do with humility? Let me expound! One morning, while standing in front of my mirror washing my face, I heard a still small, voice saying, "Call [my ex-husband] and say to him, 'I release you.'"

I remember thinking to myself, "That has got to be my mind telling me to call him. I am not going to call him. He's going to think that I want him back." Oh, my! Pride at its best! However, you must know that the word *pride* never crossed my mind at that time. So, of course, I did not call him.

But, thank God for His patience. I heard the same still, small voice the next morning, again while standing at the sink in front of my mirror, washing my face. It was early, before 7:00 a.m. I knew my ex-husband arrived at work before most of his coworkers and I had his direct phone number. So, this time—I was sure it was all by the prompting and help of the Holy Spirit—I picked up the phone, dialed the number, and of course, he answered the phone. I initially stuttered (now, I know it was pride, although I didn't think that before); however, I finally was able to say, "Hey, good morning. I am calling you because the Holy Spirit told me to call you and 'release you.'" I went into detail and said as I was directed: "Please forgive me if I did anything to you, to cause you to want to divorce me, and I forgive you for wanting to divorce me." Whew! I was sweating underneath it all. I fought the urge to say, "I don't want you to think that I am trying to get you to come back." Because that is NOT what the Holy Spirit prompted me to say. That was all Shelia

Smith's thinking. See, again—my pride, my stinking flesh, did NOT want to let him think for one second that I wanted him to come back. Sad, but, oh, how so true!

I love what Andrew Murray said in his book *Humility*, "It is our relationships to one another, in our treatment of one another, that the true lowliness of mind and the humility of heart are to be seen. Our humility before God has no value unless it prepares us to reveal the humility of Jesus to our fellowmen." You see, how could I possibly say that I love Jesus when I haven't seen him face-to-face yet? However, my ex-husband, whom I said I loved and had been married to and saw him daily for the past 25 years, how could I be so self-centered and not think for one moment that he could possibly be hurting too? God loved him just as much as he loved me and desired the best for both of us. God knew that perhaps my ex-husband needed to hear those words just as much as I needed to say them. He knew that we both needed to be set free.

My ex-husband seemed a little shocked. However, he knew me well enough to believe that if I said the

Holy Spirit told me to call him, it was enough for him to accept it, which he graciously did. God wanted me to do just as his Word declared, "Do nothing out of selfish ambition or vain conceit, but in humility consider others better than yourselves" (Phil. 2:3). God wanted me to clothe myself in compassion and humility (Col. 3:12). Please, somebody, help me say BUT GOD!

God, in His sovereignty, was working graciously with me—to help me position myself for the healing that I had been praying for. I finally got the revelation on what these words meant "…God is light, and in him, there is no darkness…" Healing could not flow through me because there was darkness blocking the passageway. And little did I know it was the sin of pride that was hiding deep within my heart; hence, the reason I was unable to get a breakthrough in my prayer. Wow! All praises to God for the Holy Spirit shining the spotlight on his Word and providing me with this revelation!

In the same online article (at the beginning of the chapter), the author stated God "will work with us when we desire humility, but the development of humility will be painful. Despite the discomfort, we find an added measure of grace to sustain us as we suffer through the refining process!" The revelation came as a result of being in a steadfast place of Prayer! —which was also moving me closer to discovering my God-given destiny for my life; however, the process was not yet over. There was more to come. Whew! I am a work in progress.

❖ *Reflections*

What are some distractions or barriers that hinder you from being effective in Prayer?

Are you able to discern the work of the Holy Spirit in your situation/time of difficulties? If not, pause and ask Him to show you His perspective in your circumstance. What is one thing you can do today, to move you closer to your God-given destiny?

Humility: Faith

But without faith, it is impossible to please him, for he who comes to God must believe that he is and that he is a rewarder of those who diligently seek him.

— Heb. 11:6 NKJV

So, what is faith? According to the writer of Hebrews 11, "Now faith is the assurance (title deed, confirmation) of things hoped for (divinely guaranteed), and the evidence of things not seen [the conviction of their reality—faith comprehends as fact what cannot be experienced by the physical senses]. For by this [kind of] faith, the men of old gained [divine] approval.

"By faith [that is, with an inherent trust and enduring confidence in the power, wisdom and the goodness of God] we understand that the worlds (universe, ages) were framed *and* created [formed, put in order, and equipped for their intended purpose] by the word of God so that what is seen was not made out of things which are visible" (1–3 AMP).

Wow! I love this translation. The first thing I notice is that faith is **NOW**! It is not in the past, nor is it in the distant future. When God speaks to us, whether it be through his Word, through dreams, visions, or whatever method He chooses, it is present tense, for the immediate, right here and right now. He expects us to not only believe what He says but to believe and receive it *Now!* God cares for us, and He is concerned about everything that concerns us (Ps. 138:8).

God knew all about me; the dizzy spells, and all the other health challenges that I was facing. God knew my ex-husband had departed; in fact, because He is all-knowing, He knew before time began that this very day would come. You may be wondering, "Did God plan for this to happen?" No, he did not! It was God who instituted marriage (Gen. 2:18–25); however, He was not caught by surprise.

We live in a broken world, and all too often, we desire to do our own thing, even at the expense of hurting others. In this situation—and in every case—God's desire was for me to acknowledge Him and to trust that He would never leave me, nor forsake me, just as He said when I was sitting on the stairwell, sobbing my eyes out the first night my ex-husband left.

The Scripture says, "Therefore humble yourselves under the mighty hand of God [set aside self-righteous pride], so that he may exalt you [to a place of honor in his service] at the appropriate time, casting all your cares [all your anxieties, all your worries, and all your concerns, once and for all] on him, for he cares about you [with deepest affection, and watches over you very carefully]" (1 Pet. 5:6–7).

It was my self-righteous pride that was getting in the way of me moving forward. God wanted me to "cast" really cast my cares upon Him. I heard someone use the example of casting a fishing rod into the deep sea. The fisherman posture himself by leaning way back, and then with all his might and strength, he throws the fishing rod out into the deep sea with high expectation of catching a fish. God was waiting for me to come down off my high horse (as

Mama Lottie would say) and to once and for all, give everything to Him.

Let's look at the second term from Hebrews 11 that stood out to me: Title deed. Merriam-Webster.com defines *Title deed* as "the deed constituting the evidence of a person's legal ownership." Let me stop right here. I wanted to underline this.

This is the perfect definition. The word of God is that legal instrument (in writing), and it confirms that I have a right (in this case, my healing) and, of course, whatever else I may need. However, since I am speaking specifically about the travails with my health during the first three to four years after my ex-husband left, my healing had been sealed by the blood of Jesus when He hung, bled, and died on that rugged cross. He rose again to life three days later, with all power and authority in His hands. Healing belonged to me. Jesus paid for healing and transferred the rights to His children (Isa. 53:5, Matt. 15:22–29, 1 Pet. 2:24).

This third phrase, *divinely guaranteed*, is powerful! You see, when God speaks a Word to us, no matter what method He chooses, it is a done deal!

It does not matter what we see, hear, think, or feel. It has been divinely guaranteed. However, we must choose to take God at His word and believe for our healing, deliverance, breakthrough, finances, or whatever the situation may be until it manifests. Faith is not faith unless we DO something. We must act, instead of wallowing in self-pity while at the same time being full of pride.

The lame man at the pool of Bethesda had been lying there for 38 years, waiting for someone to put him in the water. Jesus asked him if he wanted to be healed. He stated he didn't have anyone to put him in the pool when the waters were stirred up. Jesus simply told him to "Get up, take your bed and walk" (Jn. 5:8). I had to swallow my pride and cry out to my heavenly Father for HELP! I was in desperate need of Him. Here I was, living what I felt to be the perfect life in paradise that went from being celebrated to being shameful all in one day. Empty nest. No husband, no biological family on the island, health seemed to be failing (dizzy spells, then the female issues with hormones), and what more could happen? Next, my finances were attacked! How could I continue to live in Hawaii with no job and no salary? Only by the grace of God. I had to take up my bed and walk. I am still learning that meekness is NOT a sign of weakness. It is like a magnet that attracts the grace of God.

"But he continues to pour out more and more grace upon us. For it says, 'God resists you when you are proud but continually pours out grace when you are humble.' So then, surrender to God. Stand up to the devil and resist him, and he will turn and run away from you. Move your heart closer and closer to God, and he will come even closer to you. But make sure you cleanse your life, you sinners, and keep your heart pure and stop doubting" (Jas. 4:6–8 TPT).

❖ *Reflections*

What situation are you facing that is requiring you to put your faith in God? What do you want to admit to yourself about how you are making this choice? What are you willing to do to adjust your thinking and draw closer to God in faith?

Humility: Rest

Come to Me, all who are weary and heavily burdened [by religious rituals that provide no peace], and I will give you rest [refreshing your souls with salvation]. Take My yoke upon you and learn from Me [following Me as My disciple], for I am gentle and humble in heart, and you will find rest (renewal, blessed quiet) for your souls. For My yoke is easy [to bear] and My burden is light.

— Matt. 11:29–30 (AMP)

Reflecting and reading the words of Jesus in this passage brought tears to my eyes. He is so amazing, so loving and gentle; indeed, He is! Jesus beckons us to come to Him. He's aware of our weariness and fragility because, after all, He is the Lord God our Maker (Ps. 95:6). *Heavy labor* and *heavy yoke* are two of many other phrases used for "heavily burdened" in other translations of the Bible.

Nonetheless, I believe the connotation is clear; it is burdensome, and it provides no peace.

I don't know about you, but, unknowingly, I had slipped into the "religious rituals" mind-set that if I just do this, or if I pray for two hours a day, or if I read my Bible for four hours instead of thirty minutes, if I go to church today, or if I pay my tithes, whatever the case may have been, I just wanted the madness to stop. I felt like it was all on me to do everything just right, or else my labor was in vain.

But, we see here in the passage above that Jesus did not say any of these things (check it out in other versions/Bible translations for yourself); He simply said: "Come to Me, all who are weary and heavily burdened, and I will give you rest." He then goes on to say, "Take My yoke upon you and learn from Me." There was no doubt in my mind by this time of my journey that the cares of this world were trying to smother the life out of me. I felt like giving up.

Fast-forward…okay, so I was finally getting over the fact that my twenty-five-year marriage had ended in divorce before this word came: "Delight yourself also in the LORD, and he shall give you the desires of your heart" (Ps. 37:4 NKJV). The Holy Spirit woke me at 4:30 a.m. my first day back at work after being out for two weeks. I had been hospitalized earlier that month for a few days after a severe attack of vertigo (dizzy spells) while speaking at a National Day of Prayer event sponsored by our Protestant Women of the Chapel fellowship group. (Testimony for my next book in this series.)

I was speechless the day I returned to work when my boss informed me my job of eighteen and a half years, with a six-figure salary, was coming to a sudden end due to "downsizing middle managers." First, it was my marriage and health almost simultaneously, and now my finances were being attacked as I lost my job and was proudly living in Hawaii, the land I knew the Lord brought me to.

What was the lesson in all of this? You might ask. It took me a while before I started to put the pieces of this puzzle together. I was so fixated on the fact that if **"I"** could just regain my health, then **"I"** will be all right because **"I"** would be able to find another job.

"I" will be able to rise again; **"I"** will make it work once more! Did you notice how many times the word **"I"** was used? That was the problem: Pride. It was all on me to fix everything!

Jesus, through the precious Holy Spirit, was speaking to me every way He could; through my prayer times, through my journaling, through dreams—all because He was beckoning me to come to Him. He did not expect me to fix these issues on my own. God knew exactly where I was in life. He had promised to never leave me nor forsake me (Heb. 13:5), yet it was my pride that was keeping me from submitting and surrendering my life to His way. He eagerly desires to order our footsteps in His Word (Ps. 119:133). However, we must be willing to follow His lead and His ways.

Here's an excerpt from my journal (precisely one day before I received my pink slip).

Monday, March 27, 2006 – Time: 11:24 a.m. *Again, after my prayer and thanksgiving time, I sensed the need to read Psalm 91, and afterward, I wrote, "Trust that the LORD, God will lead and guide me into all Truth! He is my Rock, my Buckler, my Shield, and in him will I trust! God is a good God. He is my refuge in times of trouble. He is my shelter in the storm. He is my compass when I'm lost, and when I lose my direction. He is my light when I can't seem to see my way. God is a good God! He's merciful, kind, and compassionate to all who call on his Great Name! He is the Restorer of the Breach! He is the Rock of my Salvation. He is the One and Only True God! All will come to know him and reverence him! Be still and know that he is God. Take heed, lest you fall.*

I concluded the journal entry with my usual salutation-- giving him thanks for speaking to me, for Father God had spoken to me during my prayer time. He was preparing my heart to rest, even before I received the news regarding the downsizing. He told me through that prayer, *"Be still…"* So, what was the next step after coming to him? He wanted me to learn from him, for he is gentle and humble in heart. He knew what was ahead of me in the coming days. He knew my flesh would rise and try to fight the process. However, He desired that I find my rest in Him and not in the world; nor to get caught up in the pride of life. God knew before time began that I would be without a job. I was out of work for almost two years.

However, as I reflect on my experience during that time, those were the best two years of my life. The Father taught me (and still is teaching me) how to trust Him and how to rest in Him. I have so much more to share of His goodness and mercy as He gently showed me how to take up His yoke and learn from Him. My life was forever changed during this time.

Listen to what David had to say about the Father: "You saw me before I was born and scheduled each day of my life before I began to breathe. Every day was recorded in your book! How precious it is, Lord, to realize that you are thinking about me constantly! I can't even count how many times a day your thoughts turn toward me. And when I awaken in the morning, you are still thinking of me!" (Ps. 139:16–18 The Living Bible).

Wow! God knows me. He knows you. God knows us! I invite you to join me on this journey as we continue to learn how to humble ourselves and lay our life down in tender surrender before the Lord, for He has promised it will bring life, prosperity, and honor as our reward.

❖ *Reflections*

Are you weary, tired, and heavy-laden? Could pride possibly be the culprit of your inability to find rest for your soul? Jesus offers rest. According to Matthew 11:29-30, what are the three things you must do to find this rest?

The world is waiting for YOU to take your rightful place in the Kingdom and do the very thing you were created to do—bringing glory and honor to God, our heavenly Father!

I submit to you, Humility is the master key to unlocking your God-given destiny, reclaiming your Kingdom position, and living the purpose-filled life you have been searching for.

Stay tuned for the next key principle, Teachable Spirit, in this book series.

Prayer for Salvation and Baptism in the Holy Spirit

⬤ ··◆·· ⬤

Father, in the name of Jesus Christ of Nazareth, I come to you just as I am, broken in spirit and as humbly as I know-how. Your Word says, "Whosoever, shall call upon the Name of the LORD shall be saved" (Rom. 10:13). I am calling upon you to save me. I pray and ask you, Jesus, to come into my heart and be the Lord over my life, and I surrender my will and life to you. According to Romans 10:9, if I confess with my mouth, the Lord Jesus, and believe in my heart that God has raised Him from the dead, I shall be saved. For with the heart, man believes unto righteousness, and with the mouth, confession is made unto salvation. Rom. 10:10 (KJV).

So, I confess with my mouth now that Jesus Christ of Nazareth is Lord, and I believe in my heart that God raised him from the dead. I thank you, Jesus, for coming into my heart, and I am now saved. I am born again. I am a Christian, a child of the Almighty God!

Father, I also want everything that you have made available to me, now that I am your child, called by your name. According to your Word in Luke 11:13, "If you then, being evil, know how to give good gifts to your children, HOW MUCH MORE shall your heavenly Father give the Holy Spirit to them that ask him?" Based on your word, I am asking you to fill me with the Holy Spirit, rise within me as I praise God. I fully expect to speak with other tongues as you give me utterance (according to Acts 2:4). I thank you now, Father, in the name of your One and Only Begotten Son, Jesus Christ of Nazareth.

***

Now, begin to praise and thank God for being born again because you are a new creation in Christ Jesus (2 Cor. 5:17–21), and you are an heir of God and a joint-heir with Jesus Christ (Rom. 8:17). Begin to speak those words and syllables you receive—not in your native language, but the language given to you by the Holy Spirit. You must surrender your will, your tongue, and your voice to the Holy Spirit. The Holy Spirit will not force you to speak. You don't need to be concerned with how it sounds or what you sound like. It is a heavenly language! And just like a newborn baby who starts out cooing, babbling, and then speaking fluently as he practices speaking what he hears, so it is with this heavenly language. As you start to exercise your faith and articulate what you hear (the voice of the Holy Spirit), soon you will speak fluently, and you will be edified, and God will be glorified.

Prayer For Humility

Thank you, Father, that I am positioned in Christ and united in Him—and what a great comfort this is to my heart and soul. Lord, I know that I have no right to have received your amazing grace, for I acknowledge that it is against you alone that I have sinned in thought, word, and deed. Yet you saw fit to leave your heavenly throne and be born into this world of sin, as a little baby, so that by your grace and mercy, you could stoop down and pick me up and seat me together with Christ in heavenly places. Love so amazing, so divine, demands my soul, my life—my all.

And so, I kneel humbly before you and pray that by that same grace, you would finish the good work that you started in me when I trusted the Lord Jesus as my Savior. I pray that my life may reflect him and that the deep humility, meekness, and goodness that was so evident throughout his entire life may be reflected in me.

I pray that, like Jesus, I may learn obedience, even if it means having to experience suffering and pain. And, Father, I pray that, like Him, I may act justly, and have love and mercy and walk humbly with you all the days of my life, to your praise and glory, and in Jesus's name I pray. Amen.

— Author Unknown

Quiz Your Knowledge

Find a Scripture in the Bible to support your viewpoint.

1. Humility does not mean being a doormat. Can assertiveness and pride coexist? If so, explain.

2. A humble person is teachable. They don't claim to know everything. They invite feedback. They are not afraid of asking questions. True or False?

3. A humble person is not afraid to seek help. He or she sees this as an opportunity to develop, not as a sign of weakness. True or False?

4. God resists the proud but gives grace to the humble. True or False?

5. Pride comes before destruction. True or False?

6. A humble person is not afraid to celebrate the accomplishments of others because he or she

esteem others as higher than themselves. True or False?

7. A humble person is open to a personal relationship with God, the Father, Jesus Christ, His Son, and the Holy Spirit. True or False?

8. A humble person is not easily offended; is quick to forgive and full of mercy and compassion. True or False?

9. A humble person will give his or her time and attention to the lowest person or task. They do not think they are holier than thou but willingly associate with the lowly. True or False?

10. A humble person willingly submits themselves to God, prays, seeks his face, and turns from their wicked ways. True or False?

Scriptures – Humility

NKJV/NIV

James 4:10 – "Humble yourselves in the presence of the Lord, and He will exalt you."

Ephesians 4:2 – "…with all humility and gentleness, with patience, showing tolerance for one another in love.

Micah 6:8 – "He has told you, O man, what is good; And what does the LORD require of you but to do justice, to love kindness, And to walk humbly with your God."

1 Peter 3:8 – "To sum up, all of you be harmonious, sympathetic, brotherly, kindhearted, and humble in spirit."

Proverbs 16:19 – "It is better to be humble in spirit with the lowly Than to divide the spoil with the proud."

1 Peter 5:5 – "You younger men, likewise, be subject to your elders; and all of you, clothe yourselves with humility toward one another, for God is opposed to the proud, but gives grace to the humble."

Luke 1:52 – "He has brought down rulers from their thrones And has exalted those who were humble."

2 Chronicles 7:14 – "If My people who are called by My name will humble themselves and pray and seek My face and turn from their wicked ways, then I will hear from heaven, and will forgive their sin and heal their land."

1 Peter 5:6 – "Therefore humble yourselves under the mighty hand of God, that He may exalt you in due time."

Psalm 25:9 – "He guides the humble in what is right and teaches them His way."

Proverbs 18:12 – "Before destruction, the heart of a man is haughty, And before honor *is* humility."

Luke 18:14 – "I tell you, this man went down to his house justified *rather* than the other; for everyone who exalts himself will be [d]humbled, and he who humbles himself will be exalted."

Daniel 4:37 – "Now I, Nebuchadnezzar, praise and extol and honor the King of heaven, all of whose works *are* truth, and His ways justice. And those who walk in pride He is able to put down."

Proverbs 8:13: – "The fear of the Lord *is* to hate evil; Pride and arrogance and the evil way and the perverse mouth I hate."

Proverbs 15:25 – "The Lord will destroy the house of the proud, But He will establish the boundary of the widow."

Colossians 3:12 – "Therefore, as God's chosen people, holy and dearly loved, clothe yourselves with compassion, kindness, humility, gentleness, and patience."

Proverbs 11:12 – "When pride comes, then comes disgrace, but with humility comes wisdom."

Psalm 149:4 – "For the LORD takes delight in his people; he crowns the humble with victory."

Romans 12:16 – "Live in harmony with one another. Do not be proud, but be willing to associate with people of low position. Do not be conceited."

Isaiah 57:15 – "For thus says the High and Lofty One Who inhabits eternity, whose name *is* Holy: "I dwell in the high and holy *place,* With him *who* has a contrite and humble spirit, To revive the spirit of the humble, And to revive the heart of the contrite ones."

Works Cited

Amplified Bible Copyright © 2015 by The Lockman Foundation, La Habra, CA 90631. All rights reserved.

John Ankerberg Show, The. "The Fellowship of His Suffering." https://www.jashow.org/articles/the-fellowship-of-his-suffering/

Bible Exposition Commentary Volume 2, The. Wheaton, Illinois: SP Publications, Inc. VICTOR BOOKS A division of Scripture Press, 1989.

Daily Bible Study, by Wayne Blank http://www.keyway.ca/htm2002/20021231.htm

Munroe, Myles. *God's BIG Idea: Reclaiming God's Original Purpose for Your Life*. Shippensburg, PA: Myles Munroe Destiny Image Publishers, Inc., 2008.

Murray, Andrew. *Humility*. New Kensington, PA 15068: Whitaker House, 1982.

Prayer for Humility: https://prayer.knowing-jesus.com/Prayers-for-Humility#1291

Smith, Shelia A. *Simply Faith: The Birthing of a Warrior*. CreateSpace, 2017.

Title Deed.
https://www.google.com/search?client=firefox-b-1-d&q=what+is+a+title+deed%3F

"What Does the Bible Say About How to Humble Yourself?" https://www.gotquestions.org/how-to-humble-yourself.html

About the Author

Shelia Smith is, first and foremost, a daughter of Zion. She is in love with Jesus Christ, the One and Only Begotten Son of the Father, and recognizes that without Him and the Holy Spirit, she is nothing.

Shelia was born and raised in Pensacola, Florida, and moved from one paradise to another. She has lived in the beautiful island state of Hawaii for the past 32 years. She attends the Joint Base Pearl Harbor-Hickam Gospel Service and serves as a ministry leader and prayer coordinator. Shelia has been the primary leader for the Tuesday Night Women's Bible Study for the past 24 years. She has the heart to see women discover their identity in Christ Jesus as they grow in the knowledge and wisdom of God through their personal relationship with Christ empowered by the Holy Spirit. She attends a myriad of chapel functions to include Woman 2 Woman Bible Study and Women of the Chapel Fellowship Events.

Shelia is a Licensed Registered Nurse with over 37+ years of experience and serves in her community full-time. She has a passion for the lost and homeless, and those suffering from mental illnesses bound by substance abuse and demonic spirits. Shelia believes the Spirit of the Lord is upon her and has anointed her to preach the gospel to the poor, heal the brokenhearted, preach deliverance to the captives, recover sight to the blind, and set liberty to them that are bruised. She recognizes that deliverance from these strongholds is only accomplished through prayer and deliverance by the power of the Holy Spirit. Her desire is to do the work of the ministry, fulfilling what she believes to be her God-given destiny for this hour, which is to establish and maintain a healing home, "Zoe" The God-kind of Life, on the island, restoring and reconciling the captives—God's people—back to Him through His Son, Jesus Christ, the Savior.

Shelia also holds a real estate license in the state of Hawaii. She has a published article in *Trump Real Estate Magazine* (2007), noted for her success story as a first-time real estate entrepreneur enrolled in the Trump Real Estate Investment Program.

She is the proud mother of three children; two adult sons, Roderick and Oliver Jr., a stepdaughter, Lashonda Michelle Smith-Lazard; a daughter-in-law, Johnita, and four beautiful grandchildren: Rod Jr., Levi James, Ava Marie, and Layla Rose.

OTHER BOOKS BY SHELIA A. SMITH

*#1 International Best Seller- Simply Faith: The
Birthing of a Warrior © 2017*

A CONTRIBUTING AUTHOR TO:

*Called to Coach © 2018: BY Janice LaVore-Fletcher,
PCC, CMC with Donna Wyland, CPLC*